THE WAY OF THE CROSS

Five Studies based on Holy Week Addresses on the
Form and Structure of the Christian Life

By the same Author

JESUS THE MESSIAH

THE EPISTLE TO THE HEBREWS:
An Historical and Theological Re-consideration

THE GOSPEL OF LUKE:
A volume of the Moffatt New Testament Commentary

THE WAY
OF THE CROSS

Five Studies based on Holy Week Addresses
on the Form and Structure of the
Christian Life

by

WILLIAM MANSON

HODDER AND STOUGHTON

Made and Printed in Great Britain for
HODDER AND STOUGHTON LTD., by
T. AND A. CONSTABLE LTD., Printers,
Edinburgh

To my former students in Knox College, Toronto, New College, Edinburgh, and the United States of America, with my affection.

WILLIAM MANSON, D.D.

1882 — 1958

In the early hours of Good Friday 1958 Professor William Manson passed to his rest. Just a year before, throughout Holy Week 1957, he had delivered a most notable series of addresses in St. Giles' Cathedral, Edinburgh. It is these addresses which are now given to a wider public in the pages that follow.

Born at Cambuslang, William Manson had his early education at Glasgow High School, proceeding thence to Glasgow University. There by his prowess in the fields both of ancient languages and of English literature he gave early promise of future attainments; and when he graduated with First Class Honours in Classics, he was awarded a Gold Medal as the most distinguished student over the whole Arts course. After Glasgow came Oxford. Having won an Open Scholarship at Oriel, he took a First Class in Honour Moderations and a First in Greats. But long before this, he had been feeling the inward compulsion of the call to the ministry. So he returned to Glasgow and entered the United Free Church College —now Trinity College of the University—where such illustrious teachers as James Denney and George Adam Smith were revolutionising Biblical exposition and inspiring a generation of students. In 1911 he was ordained to the ministry at Oban, and three years later was called to the important charge of Pollokshields East, Glasgow.

By this time his reputation as scholar and teacher had crossed the Atlantic, and in 1919 came the offer of the New Testament Chair in Knox College, Toronto: six years there enabled him to make a contribution of lasting value to the life of the Canadian Church. But his own Church could not consent to be deprived longer of the services of one of her most distinguished sons; and in 1925 the General Assembly appointed him Professor of New Testament Language, Literature and Theology in New College, Edinburgh, where he took his place in the notable succession of Marcus Dods and H. A. A. Kennedy. After the reunion of the Scottish Churches in 1929 and the consequent agreement between Church and University, Professor Manson continued to occupy the Chair of New Testament, until in 1946 he succeeded Principal Curtis in the Chair of Biblical Antiquities and Biblical Criticism. Honorary Doctorates of Divinity were conferred upon him by both Glasgow and Toronto. A man of wide culture and a scholar of the first rank, he influenced decisively contemporary developments in British theology, particularly in the field of New Testament research and interpretation; and his writings have been acclaimed not only in this country but also on the Continent and in America. It was a fitting tribute to one of the greatest Biblical scholars of the day when he was called to the President's Chair of the *Societas Novi Testamenti Studiorum*.

Through Manson's lecture-room at New College there passed not only future ministers of the Church at home and missionaries in the field but also a great multitude of overseas students, theological undergraduates and post-graduates from many lands and Churches. What their teacher imparted to them was more than an appreciation of the integrity of Biblical scholarship or a knowledge of the methods of scientific exegesis: it was something of the exhilaration of the New Testament faith. If he was too much of a scholar to expound the Gospels and Epistles without the most careful examination of critical problems and diversities of interpretation, he was too much of an apostle to stop there, too eager an ambassador for Christ not to convey in all its breadth and length and depth and height the Gospel of reconciliation. Without a doubt, Manson was one of the most erudite Biblical interpreters of his time; but he was the humblest of men, for he was otherworldly in the true sense of that much misunderstood word, carrying with him everywhere the mystic's sense of the divine presence, and always helping duller minds to apprehend that unseen world of which he himself was so vividly aware. To hear Manson expounding Romans or St. John was to be delivered from all second-hand, superficial interpretations and facile theologising, and to be confronted again with the awe of the majesty and mystery of God. 'Put off thy shoes from thy feet, for the place whereon thou standest is holy ground.'

His book *Jesus the Messiah*, certainly one of the most significant contributions to New Testament theology in this generation, shows the balanced and discriminating judgment he brought to bear on the so-called Form Critical approach to the Gospels, making creative use of its potentialities, avoiding its excesses and extravagances; while his later volume on the Epistle to the Hebrews illustrates his questing and exploring spirit, ever hospitable to new discovery and ready to break fresh ground. But these two books, and indeed all Manson's writings—including such earler works as *Christ's View of the Kingdom of God*, *The Incarnate Glory*, and the Commentary on St. Luke—manifest characteristics even more important than penetrating judgment and the spirit of the pioneer: a constant, urgent preoccupation with the mighty acts of revelation (how often he used to say—'The only God the New Testament knows is the God of the Resurrection'!) and an intense devotion to the faith once for all delivered to the saints. His life and work have thus given a shining proof that the faith of the disciple and the vision of the mystic, often regarded as disqualifying for an objective and dispassionate exploration of the Biblical records, are in fact the indispensable equipment for a just appraisal of these records and a true understanding of their essential meaning.

Manson was no scholarly recluse, and it was his lifelong joy to serve the Church at large, particularly in the ecumenical field. He had been Convener of the Inter-Church Relations Committee of the Church of Scotland, Scottish Chairman of the Conference on Intercommunion with the Church of England, and Vice-President of the British Council of Churches. The divisions of Christendom weighed heavily on his spirit as an intimate personal concern. Always the soul of courtesy towards those whose ecclesiastical traditions differed from his own, he strove constantly for closer understanding, inspired by his longing for the breaking down of the walls of partition and by his vision of the coming fullness of the Church. Never was there a more truly ecumenical spirit than his. To be his colleague was an experience of extraordinary stimulus and encouragement. To be his friend was to see something of the lovingkindness and serenity, the integrity and gentleness of the Master Himself. Right nobly he served his generation according to the will of God; and now that he has passed beyond our sight we thank God upon every remembrance of him, rejoicing in the grace that made him so clear and so persuasive a herald of that Word which is light for this distracted age, glad tidings to the meek, and the opening of the prison to them that are bound.

JAMES S. STEWART

PREFATORY NOTE

THESE pages incorporate a series of addresses which the writer delivered in St. Giles' Cathedral, Edinburgh, in Holy Week 1957. For the kindness of the invitation to be the preacher on these occasions cordial thanks are expressed to the Rev. H. C. Whitley, D.D., Minister of St. Giles', and to the Kirk-Session.

In response to the desire that these studies might be made available for a wider audience, the writer has taken occasion to include certain expansions of an exegetical and theological nature which the subject-matter seemed to require. These expansions, like the rest of the material, keep within the general purpose of showing how the manifestation of Jesus in the flesh and His intercourse with men have historically determined the form and nature of the Christian life. To have carried the subject further, into the light of the Easter Day morning, would have required a supplementary series of studies.

A few paragraphs in one or another of the addresses have been taken over from an earlier article by the writer on 'The Norm of the Christian Life in the Synoptic Gospels' which appeared in the *Scottish Journal of Theology* for March 1950. For permission to reproduce this material indebtedness is expressed to the Editors of that Journal.

EDINBURGH, 1958.   W. MANSON.

CONTENTS

I

THE COMING OF JESUS CHRIST

*And the Word was made flesh, and dwelt among us (and
we beheld His glory, glory as of the only begotten from the
Father), full of grace and truth.* St. John 1.14

In Holy Week we stand before the supreme Events
which, with their sequel on the first Easter Day,
constitute the basis and have shaped the character of
the Christian faith.

The light falls on a meridian stage of time on
which the concluding acts of a great historical drama,
linking together past, present and future time, are
passing into fulfilment. Jesus of Nazareth, known to
the mass of His contemporaries as a prophet, though
not yet as more than a prophet, has arrived at the
Holy City for the festival of Passover, and is
acclaimed by His disciples and by other pilgrims
with wavings of palm branches and with verses
chanted from Psalm 118 which celebrate the blessed
One who comes in the name of the Lord and brings
in the reign of righteousness (Mark 11.9-10).

The next day, *Monday*, Jesus visits the Temple,
cleanses its courts of secular traffic, and protests that,
as His Father's house, the sanctuary is to be a house
of prayer for all nations (Mark 11.17).

On *Tuesday*, being interrogated by the hierarchy
and the scribes as to the ground of His authority for
so acting, Jesus reserves His answer, but in the open
parable of the Vineyard, and in other parables and

B

answers to questions, He confronts the rulers of the nation with their age-long unfaithfulness to God's requirement of obedience from His people, and warns them of the terrifying responsibility which has now come to rest on them (Mark 12.9-11), predicting also the destruction of impenitent Jerusalem and the advent of the Last Judgement of the world.

Wednesday is passed in rest and seclusion at Bethany, but on the evening of that day a woman disciple, divining the secret of Jesus and prescient of His approaching death, significantly anoints His head with costly unguent, while Judas sells Him to the authorities (Mark 14.3-11).

Events follow swiftly. On *Thursday*, at His last gathering with the Twelve, Jesus institutes the sacrament of His Body and Blood (Mark 14.12-25), and the same evening, after the agony in the garden of Gethsemane, He is arrested, brought to trial before the high priest, and upon His avowal of His divine commission as the Messiah, is condemned for blasphemy. On *Friday* He is hurried before the Roman procurator and, after being scourged and mocked, is sentenced to death on the charge of being a pretendant to Jewish kingship, the sentence being carried out by crucifixion.

I

Such in briefest outline is the drama of Holy Week, which has stirred and affected the lives of men as nothing else in human story.

A certain analogy, indeed, may be sought in the last days and death of Socrates at Athens in 399 B.C. Socrates also perished at the hands of his people for fidelity to his conscience and sense of mission, and like Jesus he repelled all suggestions to seek escape from his fate. Moreover, the death of Socrates profoundly affected the course of all later Greek thinking. It shattered both the old tradition in ethics and the shallow rationalism of the sophists, and drove philosophy in Greece to seek deeper spiritual foundations. There, however, the analogy and the resemblance end. Socrates brought to men no reconstitutive vision of life or personal revelation from God, as Jesus did, nor did he speak of redemption, individual or social, from sin. He drove the individual back on himself and on his own spiritual resources, declaring the unexamined life to be not worth living but setting up no perfect norm. His word to men was in substance the philosophical application of the Delphic adage: 'Know thyself!' Jesus, on the other hand, leads men out of themselves to God. He calls them to seek, to receive, and to make way in their lives for the *Kingdom of God*, the advent of which He has come to proclaim. That Reign or Rule of God, which in the past history of the people of Israel had been only an apocalyptic vision, a shining hope which, intermittently brightening their sky, had ever and anon receded into invisibility, is brought near in its immediate reality and in its inexorable moral requirement to the souls and consciences of men, and becomes, as Jesus presents it, an instant summons to the individual to repent and to be reconciled to God. And it is this engagement of Jesus to bring men forward out of their sinful selves into reconciliation with God that gives the final events of Passion Week their unique and critical significance.

As the Apostle Paul puts it—expressing in other words the same message of the urgent coming of the Reign of God to men—'God was in Christ, reconciling the world to Himself' (II Cor. 5.19) or, as he elsewhere says, 'The God who said, "Out of darkness light shall shine" (Gen. 1.3), has shone in our hearts to give the light of the knowledge of the glory of God in the face of Christ' (II Cor. 4.6). For St. Paul God's manifestation of Himself in the person and work of Jesus was the new 'Let there be light!' which had inaugurated the New Creation: the scarred face and wounds of the Crucified were the signal and summons to a divine transformation of life.

At the heart of the Passion-history, accordingly, we see Jesus self-revealed to His disciples as *the Way, the Truth, and the Life* (John 14.6). He is the Way because, coming to us from God, He opens the road between God and us, and between God's eternity and our temporality. He establishes a new intercourse, a new two-way traffic, between us sinners and God. As come from God, and yet as man among men on earth, He is for Christian faith at once the Manifestation of God to sinful men and, in virtue of His complete identification of Himself with us, He is the supreme Response or answer-back of our souls to God. We approach God through Him. His personal significance extends to, embraces, and covers us. All religion, indeed, as truly experienced is the response of our souls to some manifestation of God, but in the Christian religion the manifestation of God is through Jesus Christ alone: 'No one has at any time seen God; the only Son, who is on the

Father's breast, has interpreted Him' (John 1.18; cf. 14.9-10 and Heb. 1.1). And as light, when it passes through a prism, breaks into its component rays of primary colour, so the revelation of God in Christ, when it is received into human souls, breaks into *knowledge* of God on the one hand, and into the *life* of love to God and to man on the other. There is on the one hand theology, 'the word of the Cross', and on the other hand there is life, 'the way of the Cross'. Jesus Christ as the 'Way' is thus also the 'Truth' and the 'Life'.

2

We have, therefore, to recognize a theological as well as a practical meaning in the drama of the Passion, and it is important to stress its significance. *Theology* goes with the Christian religion and life, because it is one part of the gift which Jesus Christ has brought us. Indeed, the New Testament says that eternal life consists in *knowing* the Father of Jesus Christ as the true God, and in knowing Jesus Christ as His Son. It is surely fundamental to our Christian lives to have our minds engaged, taken up, and possessed by thoughts of the glory, the holiness and the love of God. As we look at the mystery of the world and of our human life, can we imagine any glory so absolute as holy love or so worthy to be accepted as the ultimate reality by which all men are judged and for which all things exist? That was clear to Plato, as well as to Jesus. But very certain it is to the Christian religious consciousness that, if such holy love is the ultimate perfection and reality underlying the universe, then Jesus Christ and Jesus

Christ alone is its measure and the clue to its character and identity, for greater love has no man than He. He, who is for His followers the Word who was made flesh and who was slain for us, has not only proclaimed the love of God as the last reality, but has given that love an intense and unparalleled personal expression. And He has humanized theology by His life and by His teaching. Christianity has, accordingly, an essentially theological ground and structure. But as the title prefixed to these addresses will have made plain, it is with the 'Way' of the Cross (*Via Crucis*), springing from the 'Word' of the Cross (*Theologia Crucis*), that we shall be particularly concerned in our meditation. How, we shall ask, did Jesus, who is the Truth, become the Way and the Life to the men whom first He gathered around Him in the flesh, and in whom is still to be found the essential type of Christian fellowship and obedience?

The Gospel of St. John summarizes the matter by saying that the effect of Christ's action was to communicate to His followers a new and heavenly *birth*. This choice of metaphor makes it plain that the new existence to which Jesus called His disciples was not a life which they could achieve or inaugurate by effort of their own, but which must come from God (John 1.12-13). The same is true if with the other evangelists, Mark, Matthew and Luke, we think of the work of Jesus as the calling of men to receive the Kingdom of God; God alone can give or produce what is His. Coming to His own people Israel, Jesus found it unreceptive of His message. Official Judaism had no wish for the new birth or Divine reign of which Jesus spoke. Official Judaism desired no birthright but that of its own historical election and Abrahamic descent, no Kingdom of God that did not take account of Israel's special privilege, and no life that was not the continuance of the life it had. But, says the evangelist, to those who did receive Him Jesus 'gave the power to become children of God, who were born, not of blood nor of the will of the flesh nor of the will of man, but of God'. Here was the authentic Israel of God, taken out of the nominal Israel, and deriving its character and title not from heredity or from environment or from human choice or virtue, but from God.

3

In our present study, therefore, which is of a preliminary character concerned with the Coming of Jesus Christ, we are thrown first upon the difference between Jesus and the current Jewish ideas of the Messianic deliverer. Here I take into my hands a book recently published by a Jewish scholar, a professor in the Hebrew University at Jerusalem and a distinguished Israeli nationalist. He is Dr. Joseph Klausner, and his book is *The Messianic Idea in Israel* (1956). There is a concluding chapter on 'The Jewish and the Christian Messiah', and this is the gist of what Dr. Klausner says:

The Jewish Messiah, he writes, 'redeems Israel from exile and servitude, and is to promote its political and economic fortunes as well as its virtues' (p. 521). 'His kingdom is definitely of this world' (p. 524). Again, the Jewish Messiah does not redeem his people by his blood, but instead he assists their redemption by his great abilities

and actions. As only 'a righteous man ruling in the fear of
God', the Jewish Messiah brings ethical perfection to the
world, but 'the progress of humanity does not depend on
him, but on humanity itself' (p. 530).

So Dr. Klausner, reviewing the Old Testament and
later Jewish teaching, finds the Jewish idea of the
Messianic salvation restricted within the compass of
an ethical programme which is very largely political
and secular in its outlook.

In an earlier work *Jesus of Nazareth* (1925), a very
noble and moving book, the same author writes of
Jesus from the Jewish point of view. He shows a
very real and wonderful sympathy with his subject,
but concludes by saying that what Jesus asked of the
Jewish people was impossible for it to give. (1) Jesus
asked that Israel should surrender its distinctive
culture and inheritance for a Kingdom of God which,
though loftily and purely conceived, was not Israel
in the historical sense, and this Israel could not do.
(2) Jesus claimed to speak from a personal knowledge of God which was above the Law, and this
again Israel could not allow. Dr. Klausner concedes
that Jesus represented a strain in Jewish piety which
was genuine and native to it, the strain of apocalyptic
enthusiasm, but he holds this strain to have been
dangerous to Israel's historical continuance. As a
result we are left with the impression that official
Judaism, which is here made the arbiter of religious
truth, has no room either for what Christianity knows
as the Cross of Christ or for what it calls the Holy
Spirit. Judaism will die, if need be, for the conserva-
tion and defence of the life it has, but will not
surrender that possession for the more abundant life

which Jesus offers in the name of the Kingdom of God. It will live by the law and tradition it has received, but not by the open revelation and operation of the transcendent principle of the love of God in the heart.

We are, therefore, on firm ground when we assert that in the two things, the Cross of Christ and the transcendent principle of the Holy Spirit, there lie the distinctive marks of the new life of Christianity and the foundations on which the Christian Church is built. And it remains that the Jesus who is placed on trial before the Jewish court for His distinctive principles is Himself a Jew, born under the Law, and that His first convinced adherents are Jews, all drawn from the tribes of Israel. It is in Jerusalem that He is hailed as the Blessed One who comes in the name of the Lord. It is supremely important, however, to remember that the evidence on which, according to the New Testament, the unique authority of Jesus rests, is everywhere divine, not human evidence. St. Peter, the first confessor, has the truth revealed to him not by human intimation or suggestion, but by the Father in heaven (Matt. 16.17). The same Apostle, preaching on the day of Pentecost, calls Israel to recognize that God has made the crucified Jesus both Lord and Christ (Acts 2.36). As a matter of fact it is made clear that, in respect of his confession, St. Peter had, to start with, no sense of 'the things of God' (Mark 8.33). In actual truth, Jesus steps on to the stage of history first as, for the mass of men, a *mystery*, unnamed and undefined, into the depths of whose consciousness even His followers do not themselves penetrate. But there is in Him from

the beginning an extraordinary sense of engagement
to bring Israel to God, and over this extraordinary
sense of mission we find the Holy Spirit stooping to
reveal to Him His destiny. Thus we read of the
baptismal vision of Jesus and the Voice from heaven,
'Thou art my Son' (Mark 1.10-11). Official
Judaism, if it should have harked back to the language
which is heard in such passages of Holy Scripture
as Psalm 2.7 or Psalm 89.27, might have discerned
in the voice 'Thou art my Son' the announcement of a King Messiah of the traditional type. But
—and here the mystery of His calling finds its
primary elucidation—Jesus found in the word the
summons not to seek glory in any form but to render
that perfect obedience to God by which alone
Satan's power was to be overthrown, and the Kingdom of God asserted (Matt. 4.1-11, Luke 4.1-15).
And it is as the obedient Son that we see Him under
the fierce light of the last week of His life and at His
trial and on the road to Calvary.

But all this indicates a very vast difference between
Jesus' sense of vocation and the function which
current Jewish expectation had assigned to the
Messiah. And indeed the world, as Jesus saw it, was
a very different one from that in which Israel had
thought to find deliverance by the coming of a King.
The time had gone by when for the masses of men
in Judea the salvation of God could be envisaged as
coming by earthly or political process. The older
idea turned on domination of earthly foes. But now
sin, sorrow, despair, derangement, the oppression of
mind caused by psychical ills of many kinds, largely
associated with demonic forces, had taken the place

of the old national enemies of Israel as the real oppressors of the people of God, and the salvation of God, if it came to suffering humanity, must come as liberation and redemption from the calamities and distortions caused by these spiritual powers. Simultaneously we find, in the two centuries preceding the coming of Jesus, that in certain religious circles both among the Pharisees and elsewhere a supernatural, heavenly figure, the 'Son of Man', had risen above the horizon in place of the national Messiah, and had drawn wistful thought and expectation towards himself. It is to be noticed that Jesus, on occasions when the disciples or others confessed Him to be, or inquired whether he was, the Messiah of Israel's expectation, answered in terms which displaced the title of the 'Christ' by the title of the 'Son of Man'. Thus when St. Peter at Caesarea Philippi acclaimed Him as the Christ, we read that Jesus from that moment began to unfold to His disciples the destiny of suffering appointed for the *Son of Man* (Mark 8.31), and when at His trial the high priest inquired whether He was the Christ, the Son of the Blessed, Jesus answered: 'I am, and you will see the Son of Man sitting at the right hand of Power and coming with the clouds of heaven' (Mark 14.61-62).

It is to be noticed, however, that in the prophetic Book of Daniel, which is the source of this language, the heavenly figure who wears the form of a son of man, and who is said to receive from *God* an everlasting kingdom and dominion (Dan. 7.13-14), stands symbolically for 'the saints of the Most High', that is, for the faithful remnant of Israel (Dan. 7.18, 22.27, etc.). Therefore in the choice of the term Son of Man by Jesus to designate His special function, no rejection in substance of the Jewish hope of the divine salvation is implied. Nevertheless, the preference of the term not only indicates that the Kingdom which Jesus seeks comes from *God*, but reflects and signifies that association of Himself with humanity sinful and suffering, towards which His complete obedience to God as the Beloved Son impelled Him. The prediction in Daniel gave Him language by which, both in His teaching of the disciples and in His answer to the high priest's question at His trial, His extraordinary sense of divine engagement to bring Israel to God could be stated.

We may say, then, that despite the difference between Jesus and the traditional figure of the Jewish Messiah, it was the Messianic hope of Judaism that furnished the first inevitable language in which the mystery of Jesus disclosed itself both to His own mind and to the minds of His disciples. Jewish Messianic terminology was the primary medium or reagent, as we may say, through and by which the colour and character of His unique sense of mission were brought out and conveyed. Yet the significance of Jesus and of His coming among men was destined to be expressed in even higher terms than these.

4

At this point we look for a moment beyond the events of Passion Week, though not beyond the teaching of the New Testament as a whole. An even higher language than the Messianic is demanded for the purpose of interpreting Jesus to the *world*.

As the Christian gospel passes out from Judea into the larger world, we find the terms Messiah, Christ, Son of God (in the purely Messianic sense and Son of Man making room by their side for vaster titles, namely, *Son of God* (in the absolute personal sense), *Wisdom of God* and *Word* (or *Logos*) *of God*. These terms so expand the significance of Jesus that His work as Lord and Saviour of men is brought into relation with every province of human thought and life, and in such a way as to bear upon the structure and substance of the world itself. For example, St. John begins his Gospel by speaking of the eternal Word (*Logos*) of God who was with the Father (1.1), and who became flesh and dwelt among men (1.14). Even before that Gospel was written, we find St. Paul speaking of Jesus Christ, the Son of God, in the following terms:

> He is the image of the invisible God, the first-born of all creation. In Him all things were created, in the heavens and on the earth, things visible and things invisible. . . . All things were created through Him and for Him. And He is before all things, and in Him all things hold together (Col. 1.15-17).

Similarly, the writer of the Epistle to the Hebrews states that through His Son God made the world, and says of Him:

> He reflects the glory of God and bears the very stamp of His nature, upholding the universe by His word of power (Heb. 1.3).

Here is a language derived not from the older Messianic tradition but from the Jewish *Wisdom* theology as that theology finds expression in Proverbs

8.22-31 and in post-canonical writings like Ecclesi-
asticus 24.1-12 and Wisdom of Solomon 7.22-8.1.
Things said in the Wisdom-literature about the
personified figure of the pre-existent Wisdom of God
are taken over and applied to the historical Jesus
Christ in order that the Christian apostles and
evangelists may communicate to the wider world a
full sense of what they believe to have been shown
or signified to mankind in the person and work of
the Man of Nazareth. The Greek world was seeking
wisdom, and the apostles present the Crucified
Christ as God's answer to that quest: 'For Jews
demand signs and Greeks seek wisdom, but we
preach Christ Crucified, a stumbling-block to Jews
and an irrationality to Gentiles, but to those who are
called, both Jews and Greeks, a Christ who is the
power of God and the wisdom of God' (I Cor. 1.22-
24). Specially remarkable is the language of the
Fourth Evangelist:

> The Word became flesh and dwelt among us, and we
> beheld His glory, glory as of an only Son from the Father,
> full of grace and truth (John 1.14).

The Jesus of Nazareth and Galilee and the trial-hall
and Calvary is here proclaimed to the world as the
Logos of God, as God's Self-utterance to men, as
God's Language and living Thought, as God's
Eloquence, as God's Truth in Action, as the
measure of God's Mind, nay, as One who, in His
human life and suffering, is yet to be hailed as

> God's presence and His very self
> And essence all Divine.

In the past God had said many things to the world

through prophets and holy men of God, but now His very being, mind and will have been *embodied* in the lowly, suffering, self-forgetting humanity of Jesus, which has given a new character and dimension not only to the Christian understanding of life but to the nature of the world itself. As incarnating the Word of God to man by which the world was made, Jesus and His message stand in significant and substantive relation not merely to man's spiritual nature, and not only to the Church's liturgical and devotional life, but to the whole range of what we call the world's secular interests and activities—the realms of science, art, industry, politics, and so forth. Jesus Christ and His message have import and meaning for all of these provinces of life. That is the teaching of the New Testament in its apostolic message to mankind.

5

Yet the Jesus to whom the New Testament attaches all this vast significance came to the world in humiliation. Amid the events of Passion Week He stands before us in the pure glory of His moral and spiritual humanity. Messiah of Israel? Yes, but in a manner quite undreamt of!

> Hath He marks to lead me to Him
>   If He be my Guide?
> In His feet and hands are wound-prints,
>   And His side!
>
> Is there diadem, as Monarch,
>   That His brow adorns?
> Yea, a crown in very surety,
>   But of thorns!

It is by the *paradox* of this manifestation of the Christ that the glory of God is revealed and the new birth of the Church is effected.

Very clearly does the New Testament religion set forth the aspects of our Lord's significance:

(*a*) He is the ground of the Christian assurance of forgiveness (Acts 10.38 f.; II Cor. 5.19), because He has died for our sins according to the Scriptures (I Cor. 15.3; Rom. 8.3; I Pet. 3.18) and has reconciled us to God (II Cor. 5.19). And He who is the Expiation of our sins (Rom. 3.25; I John 2.2.) will also appear again as our Judge (II Cor. 5.10; Matt. 25.31 ff.).

(*b*) His coming marks the fulness of the times, the consummation of religious history, the culminating point of divine-human relations towards which the law and the prophets had pointed (Mark 1.14-15; Matt. 5.17-18, 13.17; Luke 16.16; Rom. 3.21 ff.; Gal. 4.4-7; Acts 17.30-31; Heb. 1.1 f.), and from which the New Creation dates.

(*c*) Through Him, by His victory over sin and death (Rom. 8.3-4; Col. 2.13-15), a whole new world of spiritual gifts, powers and blessings from God—righteousness, peace, sonship, freedom, the Holy Spirit, all of these being gifts and powers of the World to Come—have been opened to us (Rom. 3.21-26, 5.1 ff.; Gal. 3.25-26; Heb. 6.4-6), and the overthrow of all forces opposed to God and His Kingdom has been assured (I Cor. 15.25; Rom. 8.35-39).

(*d*) He is the personal Revealer of God, the proof of the Love of God (Rom. 8.31-32; John 3.16; I John 3.1 f.; Rom. 5.8), the instrument of the Power

of God (I Cor. 1.23), the source of the Knowledge
of God (I Cor. 1.23; II Cor. 4.6; John 1.18; I John
1.2, 5.20), the bearer and guarantor of Eternal Life
(John 3.16, 17.3; I John 1.2).

It is important as, remembering all this, we face
again the events of Holy Week, that we should look
back to the first step in the incarnate self-manifesta-
tion of Jesus on which our faith is built. John the
Baptist has put the trumpet to his lips on the banks
of Jordan, and is calling Israel to repentance in view
of the approach of the divine Judgement. Jesus of
Nazareth, yet unknown to history, hears the call and,
going down to the Jordan, takes a place among the
penitent sinners gathered on the water's edge. Why
so? The answer can only be known by the sequel,
but from that sequel it can be seen that here, in His
first public act, Jesus is already making Himself one
with His nation in its sinfulness, putting Himself in
the ranks and in the situation of sinners, taking their
case upon Himself. Surely we may see in this action
the historical ground on which the Baptist in St.
John's record is said presently to direct two of his
followers to the baptized Jesus with the words:
'Behold the Lamb of God who takes the (load of the)
sin of the world' (John 1.29).

So Jesus is initiated into His representative and
vicarious function. As He ascends from the water,
heaven opens over Him. It is the sign of a divine
revelation to Him. He sees the Spirit like a dove
descend upon Him. He hears the Voice: 'Thou art
my Son, the Beloved; with Thee I am well pleased'
(Mark 1.11). The Voice brings to Jesus the sense
of the Father's acceptance of Him and intimates the

c

character of the office now appointed for Him. The language is Jewish and Messianic. Israel the nation had been called to be God's Son (Exod. 4.22-23; Hosea 11.1), and over the anointed and enthroned kings of Israel had been pronounced in a special sense the word: 'Thou art my Son' (Psalm 2.7; cf. Psalm 89.27). But neither Israel nor Israel's kings had achieved that complete obedience to God in which Jesus saw that sonship to God was to be realized. Pride, vainglory, selfishness and hypocrisy, indeed all forms of iniquity, had corrupted these sons and retarded and prevented the restoration among men of the lost Image of God. Prophetic Israel had been dismayed by the failure of its kings. Now in perfect obedience to the Father's will, in complete commitment and surrender of Himself, Jesus steps into the office of the Son to fulfil it even to death. 'Lo, I come to do Thy will, O God.'

It was to restore the Divine Image in man that Jesus came.

How the office was fulfilled, in familiar intercourse with men, will be the subject of our subsequent studies.

PRAYER

ALMIGHTY FATHER, *who didst manifest Thyself to Thy people Israel as the Lord God, merciful and gracious, and didst take that people into covenant with Thyself, laying on it Thy law and making known Thy promises; and who, when the fulness of the time was come, didst perfect Thy redeeming purpose by the manifesting of Thy Son, the Eternal Word; grant that as He for our sakes became flesh, and was made man, and in our nature overthrew the power of sin and death, we may receive into our hearts the wonder of this revelation, though in its height and depth and length and breadth it is beyond us, and may put our hands to the tasks of faith to which Thou hast called us, not doubting Thy power, and so finally in this world of conflict find the peace which passes knowledge; through the same Jesus Christ our Lord.   Amen.*

II

FELLOWSHIP WITH CHRIST

Jesus came into Galilee, preaching the gospel of the kingdom of God, and saying, The time is fulfilled, and the kingdom of God is at hand; repent ye, and believe the gospel. Now as He walked by the sea of Galilee, He saw Simon, and Andrew his brother . . . and Jesus said unto them, Come ye after Me, and I will make you to become fishers of men. St. Mark 1.14-17

ACCORDING to our Gospel sources, Jesus at His baptism was, as we have seen, apprised by a voice from heaven which revealed to Him His destiny. It was in the form of the intimation: 'Thou art my Son, the Beloved; in Thee I am well pleased'. We saw that in its ultimate interpretation this experience may be understood as signifying that, as the obedient Son of the Father, Jesus was to restore the Divine Image in man and to reverse the work of Satan. So at any rate the New Testament in its working out of the matter presents the meaning of the call.

With the divine voice ringing in His heart, the Jesus who confronts us in the events of Passion Week had gone on from the Jordan to face Satanic trial in the wilderness and to enter on His Galilean work. The temptation in the wilderness turned upon the meaning of His office as 'the Son of God'. What did it signify for Jesus to receive and to fulfil a destiny like this? 'Son of God' could be understood (cf. Psalm 2.7) as an ancient historical designation of Israel's anointed king, but what did such a calling imply? Did it mean, as contemporary opinion in many Jewish circles held, that the promised Messiah the Anointed of God, when He appeared, was to repeat the wonders of the Exodus and to give His people miraculous bread like the manna which Moses gave to Israel? or to bedazzle His contemporaries with signs like the *protégé* of heaven spoken of in Psalm 91.11-12? or to subject the kingdoms of the world to His rule as Scripture seemed to say the Messiah was ordained by divine decree to do (Psalm 2.8-9)? Jesus turned from each and all of these suggestions as demonic distortions of the method and purpose of the divine salvation, as in reality ways in which Satan was trying to turn the Messianic idea to his own ends. He saw God's appointed will for Him taking shape only by that perfect trust, complete submission, and fullest reverence for the Father's will which was connoted by the call to Sonship. 'Man', He answered, 'shall not live by bread alone, but by every word that proceeds from the mouth of God.' God's will for man must be seen in the totality of His revelation and of His grace. Man must not, therefore, tempt God by tearing a text of Holy Scripture from its context and seeking to impose his own will on God, nor must he derogate in any way from the reverence and obedience which are due to Him (Matt. 4.1-11; Luke 4.1-12). On this note the wilderness temptation had ended.

Now, in the last tremendous days of Jesus' life, the Voice by which He was called, the severe testing He had endured, and the men whom He had drawn to His side as He entered on His Galilean work, are all present to His mind. The Voice is there because, when in the trial-hall the high priest asks Him 'Art thou the Christ, the Son of the Blessed?' Jesus answers 'I am' (Mark 14.62). The Satanic temptation is there, because when His foes arrest Him in the garden, Jesus says to them, 'This is your hour, and the power of darkness' (Luke 22.53; cf. John 14.30). And very specially the men whom He had chosen are in His mind and heart in these last days of His life: 'You', He says, 'are they who have continued with Me in My trials, and as My Father appointed a kingdom for Me, so do I make appointment for you,' etc. (Luke 22.28, 31-37). In the present study we are to think particularly of the calling of those men.

Jesus, entering on His Galilean work, had taken two steps. On the one hand He had started preaching a message to His times. Simultaneously He had laid the foundation of a body of disciples to be with Himself. As enmity to His message and person developed, He was to draw these associates more and more closely to His side (Mark 3.6-7, 13-14). It was His wish not to work in solitariness but as the head of a fellowship of men destined to form the nucleus of a new Israel of God.

I

The message of Jesus is given by St. Mark in the summary form: 'The time is fulfilled, and the kingdom (or reign) of God has come near. Repent, and believe the glad tidings' (Mark 1.15). Jesus spoke of a certain *time* as having now fully come. The time was the appointed time, the long-predicted time, the final time at which the heavenly or supernatural

Reign of God was to appear. Prophets and kings and righteous men had desired to see that time, but had not seen it (Matt. 13.16-17; Luke 10.23-24). Jesus, conscious of the call 'Thou art my Son', now said that this promised time was at the door.

Let it be remembered that under the pressure of an ever-increasing awareness of the holiness of God in the minds of the prophets of Israel (cf. Isa. 6.1 ff.) an ever-deepening shadow of guilt had come to throw itself over Israel's moral life, and an interrogation-mark had affixed itself to all its national institutions, at least for all purer minds. The *Righteousness* of God, for example, the realization of the divine sovereignty in and for the salvation of Israel, appeared to be withdrawn from present existence. But, as the faithfulness of the Covenant-God could not be questioned by the prophets, the realization of what was wanting under the existing sinful conditions of the time was projected into the *future*, and there is built up the vision of a day or a time, in which God's purpose to bring to light His saving will for His people will be fulfilled. Into this future age or appointed time is thrown forward the hope of Righteous Nation, Righteous Ruler, Knowledge of God, the outpouring of the Spirit of God on men, the institution of a New Covenant with God, in short, the accomplishment of the final Reign of God. The prophets Jeremiah and Ezekiel in particular had proclaimed the coming of this era. Thus the former of these seers represents the God of Israel as saying to His people, after the heavy judgements that have fallen upon them for their sins: 'I know the thoughts that I think towards you, thoughts of peace and not

of evil, to give you *a latter end and hope*' (Jer. 29.11).
And again: 'Behold, the days come, saith the Lord,
that I will raise to David a righteous Branch, and he
shall reign as king . . . and this is the name by which
he shall be called, "the Lord is our Righteousness"'
(Jer. 23.5-6). In one way or another this future hope
had come to dominate the mind of later Israel.

To the contemporaries of Jesus, however, the
Reign of God of which He spoke remained largely
a hope. It was at best a dream, an apocalyptic vision
which had flitted before their minds as the rainbow
flits before the traveller. Jesus said it was NOW, this
Reign of God, this order of salvation, this Kingdom
of the End. He said it was instant, it was NEAR. But
how near? So near that now, when Jesus speaks of it
to men, it comes to fill the whole horizon of the
hearers and to dominate all their thoughts. So near
that it is now to lay its arrest on every life, to become
the one subject of concern, and to leave the hearers
no option but to accept this immediate sway of God
or to cast their lives away. No man, Jesus said, could
serve two masters (Matt. 6.24; Luke 16.13). No
man who put his hand to the plough, and looked
back, was fit for the Kingdom of God (Luke 9.62).
Jesus made God's will to reign a directly personal
and immediate issue. What did it mean for a man
that God's order of life should come to him now in
the present, and come in the absoluteness of its
holiness? Jesus asked that question, and in the
pressure of the question lay the real 'nearness' of the
Kingdom, the issue which, we may say, divides the
world B.C. from the world A.D.

We should remember that, in the Old Testament,

whenever it is said that the Lord is King, the thought of God's enemies is in the background. So it is, for example, in many of the Psalms which celebrate the Lord's sovereignty. Therefore, when Jesus proclaims that the Reign of God is at hand, it means—this had been made particularly clear in Jewish religious thought in the age preceding Jesus—that Satan's power over man's life is to be overthrown, which means in turn that sin, self-will, sensuality are to be cast out along with Satan. What would this mean for the men to whom Jesus spoke? What indeed does it mean for *any* man, Peter or Andrew, James or John, you or me, that God's Reign should come now, and come to us with this expulsive power? Jesus said REPENT! Repentance was necessary and fundamental. But how can a man repent? How achieve a new direction of his soul to God? He can *turn* indeed towards God, and that is all-essential. But beyond that, what? Can a man effect his own *deliverance* from evil? Can he give himself a new mentality, or a new will, or a new heart? The answer is, he cannot, any more than he can lift himself into the stratosphere by his shoe-strings. The effort of a man to complete the moral transformation of his nature, especially in view of the searching light of the divine holiness which Jesus Christ turns on to him, can only bring him to *despair*. But if it is not we by ourselves who are to effect this deliverance and to bring this change about, but *God*, if the first of all the Beatitudes is for 'the poor in spirit', those who in self-despair cast themselves upon God, what then? Jesus did not preach that men were to produce conversion of themselves, but he did say that God meant to reign, and that things impossible with men were possible with God (Mark 10.26-27). The part of men was to make themselves over to God, whose will it was now to bring in His kingdom, and who could be trusted to make known His power. Christianity is not virtuosity, a fine achievement of the human spirit's own producing. Christianity is for those who will give themselves up, who will abandon themselves to God that God may act. The message of Jesus is not repent *simpliciter*, but repent and believe in the gospel! Listen to the good news I am telling you! God means to bring in His reign. His is the kingdom and the power and the glory. Your part is to commit your souls to Him. As we go on, we shall see that this message means that in God's purpose Jesus has come to make Himself one with us and so to *become* our righteousness and our life. We pass on, therefore, to the theme of Fellowship with Christ.

2

The men whom Jesus chose as disciples were called to be sharers of His life. The Manifestation of God which was to be made to them was to consist in the daily, hourly, continual pressure of Jesus on their lives. This experience was mediated to these first followers through the flesh of Jesus. They heard, they saw with their eyes, they touched with their hands the Word of life (I John 1.1). To others, including ourselves, the manifestation is by means of the Holy Spirit working on us through the Gospel. According to the pattern of the religious life which here opens before us, Christians begin and go on in fellowship of life with Jesus, and as scholars in His school. They are witnesses of His actions, hearers of His words, associates of His fortunes, companions of His way, and confidants of His mind on matters relating to God, His kingdom and His salvation. Here lies the first stage in the Christian way, and it constitutes a career of wonderful privilege. It is the gracious calling of the Lord, but it is also a very searching and disturbing experience. Jesus on one occasion alludes to these disciple-followers under the figure of the 'friends of the Bridegroom', guests invited to have part in a wedding-feast (Mark 2.19). That is a very remarkable privilege. It means that, because they belong to Jesus, these followers enter with Him on the freedom and joy and on all the conditions of the *Messianic time*. They do not as yet know that the Jesus who has called them to share His lot is the Messiah of Israel, but their Master knows, and speaks and acts accordingly. For this reason, as certain parables now make plain—the parables of the New Patch on the Old Coat (Mark 2.21), the New Wine in the Old Skins (Mark 2.22), and the Guest without the Wedding Garment (Matt. 22.11-14)—these followers of Jesus are called to put on the life of the New Age, and not to go about in the old clothes of Judaism. It may be that the words about the Old Coat and the Old Wineskins were originally spoken by Jesus with sympathetic reference to the followers of John the Baptist who, as the context makes plain, were still adhering to the practice of fasting which Pharisaic righteousness prescribed. It was not to be expected that these disciples of John could adopt or share the freedom to which, in this particular matter, the followers of Jesus were summoned. However that may be, it is plain that a line is drawn by Jesus between an older era of religious practice—'The law and the prophets till John' (Luke 16.16; cf. Matt. 11.12)—and the new era of the proclaimed Kingdom of God. One who claims to exercise a higher authority than the Scribes has stepped on to the stage and points to an enlargement of life and freedom which the previous age of religion had not known.

For the same reason, as they presently learn, these disciples of Jesus are given the privilege, but also the responsibility, of receiving into their minds and hearts the 'mystery' of the Kingdom of God (Mark 4.11-12). To other people, described as 'those outside', this Reign of God, as Jesus declares its nature and its coming, remains enveloped or shrouded in 'parables'; it remains, that is to say, a figure of speech, an imaginative vision, a 'myth' as we would say, or as a dream when one awaketh. But for those whose eyes Jesus has opened to the truth, to whom He has made the Reign of God personal and inward and immediate and dominant, the situation is different. Such followers have come already under the power and within the domain of the supernatural Kingdom. Its secret has been revealed to them, and if they now share with Jesus the joy and freedom of its higher life, they must also know with Him its *pain*.

It is indeed a very disconcerting experience, as well as the blessedest of callings, to have the Manifestation of God thus made to them at close quarters, to experience it in their daily walk of life with the

Son of Man, and in the process to have the covering taken from their eyes that has hid not only God from them, but the truth about themselves. We do not know everything that passed in intimate converse between Jesus and the men whom first He called into fellowship with Himself. There must have been unrecorded hours when, taking one or another aside to be alone with Him, Jesus pointed out just what was coming between their souls and the power of God. At any rate, revealing episodes occur like St. Peter's breakdown by the lake-shore when, falling on his knees, he cries to Jesus: 'Depart from me; for I am a sinful man, O Lord!' (Luke 5.8). It is not at all a comfortable thing, in the Fellowship of Christ, to be continually searched and known to be exposed and found wanting, to be made to realize day by day how wrong we are and how far from God. It is far easier, like Peter, to wish to contract out of the pain of such self-discovery, as Peter would have done if Jesus had not been at his side, and if His strong arm and word had not stayed him. To avoid the light is natural and instinctive to men, and to face into it is hard—but it is *Life*!

And to have not only our positive errors exposed, but our deficiencies! It is not at all composing to live with the Sermon on the Mount in our ears and before our minds, to rise with it in the morning and to go to bed with it at night, to listen to what is said by Jesus about the blessedness of the unassuming and the unselfseeking, the pure in heart, the loving and the reconcilers, and then to compare all this with the kind of persons we know ourselves to be. Far easier to avoid this painful application to our lives of the high tests of the Master's word, but again, to bear this inquisition is *Life*! So again, it is not very pleasant for Peter when, on the very day he confesses Jesus to be the Christ, he finds himself caught out in the act of diverting his Master from going on to face His destiny at Jerusalem and earns the rebuke of Jesus, being told that he has a radically ungodly mind. It is not at all comforting for a follower of Jesus to be told that he has no sense of the things of God, to hear the word 'Get thee behind Me, Satan!', to realize, just when he thinks himself most shrewd and rational, that he is Satan's dupe! Yet it is in this remorseless way and for these remorseless purposes that the curriculum of Fellowship with Jesus Christ proceeds and runs its course, even for us who are less than the Apostles. The way of life lies through the light, not by circumventing it or by turning back.

3

For in the end these disciples are to go out into the world with a special charge and mission to their fellow-men. They are to function as 'the salt of the land' and as 'the light of the world' (Matt. 5.13-14). Doubtless, as fishermen, the early members of the group knew the saving and curative properties of salt, and the disappointment it would occasion if a spurious or inferior product were offered to them in the market. And doubtless, in the same calling, they knew the importance of a shore light, the beam that shone across the waters on a murky night from lamps in villages or towns set high above the lake. Similar are the purposes to be served by the followers of Jesus when He sends them forth (Mark 3.14).

But what are the spiritual qualities signified in the metaphors of salt and light? A glance at the warning words of Jesus in Mark 9.50 and Luke 14.25-35 will help to settle the question of the 'salt' which the followers of Jesus are to 'have' in themselves. Clearly in both these passages what Jesus asks is a readiness to accept sacrifice, a willingness on the part of disciples to surrender their own wills for the sake of Himself and the gospel. By the possession and the putting into practice of this sacrificial quality they will, like salt, penetrate and influence the life of society by a principle of eternal worth, a something which will induce in men a fuller capacity to receive and respond to the offer of eternal life.

As for the 'light' which they are to offer to men, we may recall words of Jesus like the saying 'If your eye is single', that is, if your vision is not distorted by selfish or divided aims, 'your whole body will be full of light' (Matt. 6.22). Jesus asks for a single-hearted devotion to God. This is the thing which will make His followers in their own persons a revelation and a guiding light to men, which will open blind eyes to the spiritual world. Their power to illumine will be proportionate to the clarity with which they receive and pass on the knowledge which has come to them in their fellowship of life with Jesus.

It is well, as we meditate in these days on Passion Week, that we should realize afresh the nature of that fellowship with Jesus Christ in which the foundations of the Christian life are laid. The Christian life as the Way of the Cross comes by the interpenetration of Christ's life and ours. Fundamentally it is the learning of the truth in the School of Christ, the acceptance of His way for our way, of His life for our life.

> O Lord, Thou hast searched me, and known me.
> Thou knowest my downsitting and mine uprising,
> Thou understandest my thought afar off.
> Thou searchest out my path . . .
> And art acquainted with all my ways . . .
> Thou hast beset me behind and before,
> And laid Thine hand upon me.   (Psalm 139.1 ff.)

The time was to come when the term 'disciples' as a name for the members of the Christian fellowship was to drop out of official use and to be replaced by other names. Already at Antioch the disciples, we are told, became known as 'Christians' (Acts 11.26). But though the name ceased to be a formal description, of the adherent to the Christian society the reality of the disciple-life remained. In a noble passage of the Epistle to the Ephesians (4.20-21) the writer, after alluding to the sins which degrade the life of Gentile society, says to his Christian readers: 'But you have not so learned the Christ'! *Learned the Christ*, he says, and then explains his meaning thus: 'If, that is, you have heard Him and have been taught by Him, as the truth is in Jesus.' Here is the disciple idea still, and here still in discipleship is the basis of the new nature, to which the same writer presently recurs, when he says: 'Put on the new nature, which after God is created in righteousness and true holiness' (Eph. 4.24).

Christ becomes our Saviour by being first our Teacher. But because the truth imparted is so particular and so intimate and so personal and searching, it is impossible to think of it as a mere communication of ideas. It is rather the communication of a living Spirit, the impact on us of a personal Life. In its personal character the teaching is the verification in Christian experience of the evangelist's formulation that in Jesus 'The Word was made flesh and dwelt among us'. The teaching of Jesus is not something which, going forth from the Speaker, can like a system of ideas be taken by itself and weighed and evaluated in abstraction from the Speaker. It is the expression of a Mind which is not exhausted by the particular words spoken on this or that occasion, but which by the very character of these occasional words points forwards to infinite reserves of further undisclosed meaning by which a permanent dependence of our souls on Him is established. This comes out very clearly at a point in the Johannine record of the ministry, when many Jewish hearers were falling away from Jesus, and Jesus puts to the Twelve the question: 'Will you also go away?' Peter answers: 'Lord, to whom can we go? Thou hast the words of eternal life' (John 6.68). Jesus had made an impression on the inner circle of followers which left it no longer thinkable that they should find in another teacher or another teaching a conceivable way to God. So also on the last day of Holy Week, when He stood before the high priest and the high priest asked Him about His disciples and His teaching, our Lord referred His questioner to the public character of His teaching. 'I have spoken openly to the world; I have always taught in synagogues and in the temple.' Then, as the final court of appeal in the matter, He pointed to His disciples,

D

and said: 'Why do you ask Me? Ask those who have
heard Me, what I said to them. *They know what I
said*' (John 18.19-21).

PRAYER

LORD JESUS CHRIST, *who didst come among men
preaching that the Kingdom of Heaven had drawn near,
give us grace to apprehend the instancy of this message,
and so to submit our lives to Thy searching, that we may
both receive for ourselves and show forth to others that
Eternal Life which Thou bestowest, for Thy name's
sake.   Amen.*

III

THE OVERCOMING OF SELF

And He called unto Him the multitude with His disciples, and said unto them, If any man would come after Me, let him deny himself, and take up his cross, and follow Me. For whosoever would save his life shall lose it; and whosoever shall lose his life for My sake and the gospel's shall save it. For what doth it profit a man, to gain the whole world, and forfeit his life? For what should a man give in exchange for his life? St. Mark 8.34-37

In what relation does the Christian life stand to nature and the order of the world? We have seen that life taking shape in Fellowship with Jesus Christ and by the interpenetration of His life and ours. We have now to notice that, in the teaching which Jesus gave about God, God and His love are brought into the most intimate and constant connection with the physical as well as with the spiritual element in human life. Everywhere, but especially in His parables, we find the most varied and lively interest in men's secular callings and activities. Nowhere does a word suggest disparagement of ordinary mundane occupations or affairs. The 'world' which is contrasted with the true life of the soul is not the physical realm in which men's energies are deployed but the moral complex of the selfish instincts and concerns which dominate men's hearts. Whereas philosophers in the Greek world had despised mundane affairs, and thought to find God by turning altogether from material to spiritual reality, Jesus has linked the being of God with the whole natural and human process, finding room in His thought for the bird on the wing and the flower in the field, for the sunshine and the rain and the growth of the seed, for man's need of bread and his need of health, and for the whole variegated pattern of human relationships and duties. God, just because He is God, is interested in all the multiform life of the world, and indeed the human panorama serves Jesus at many points as offering analogies to the order of grace. Nevertheless, with all this positive relation of His teaching to creation and humanity, and with all His intense compassion towards suffering, sorrow, and need in every form, there remains a distance between nature and grace in His teaching; and we cannot overlook, least of all in Passion Week, that between Jesus Christ and the world as men have made it there stands the stark and irreducible fact of the Cross! What now is the nature and the cause of this opposition?

With this question we come to a second stage in the unfolding of the Christian way of life. Hitherto the call of Master to disciple has been simply 'Follow Me!' Come, and you will see! Come, and you will know! But when Jesus, by this time confessed by His followers as the Christ, sets His face to go to Jerusalem to put His work to the final test at the centre of the nation's life, there strikes into His teaching, as presented in the records of St. Mark and the other Evangelists, a note not heard before. He tells His followers that He is to encounter opposition and death. The Messiah, whom they have confessed, is no other than the suffering *Servant of the Lord* of whom the Book of the Prophet Isaiah had said that he is to meet contumely and reproach and to give his life as a sacrifice for men.

In a series of remarkable utterances (Isa. 42.1-7, 49.1-7, 50. 4-9, 52.13-53.12), the great prophet of the Exile had delineated the calling and fortunes of the 'Servant of the Lord'. While in certain of the passages the latter is more or less identified with the nation of Israel itself, in others he is differentiated by the unique character of his office, and stands out in high relief from that people. There is committed to him a special mission to Israel and to the world, in terms of which he effectuates and indeed embodies a 'covenant' of God with Israel and becomes also a light to the 'Nations' (42.6, 49.5-6). He discharges this function by his perfect faithfulness to God's word and his complete acceptance for God's sake of outrage inflicted on him at the hands of men (50.4-9). Finally, by vicarious suffering carried to the point of death, he becomes an *'asham'* or sin-offering for the 'many', through which the 'many' attain to justification before God (52.13-53.12). While there is no convincing evidence in Judaism that this figure of the Servant was understood to mean the *Messiah* before the time of Jesus, Jesus now makes the identification. He interprets the Son of Man's destiny in terms of the Servant's fortunes. The Son of Man is to suffer and to be an outcast (Mark 8.31, 9.12,31). The Son of Man is to give His life as a ransom for 'many' (Mark 10.45). And, scarcely waiting for the recovery of His followers from their first dismay at this announcement, Jesus says: 'If any man will come after Me, let him deny himself, and take up his cross, and follow Me!' That is, let him say No to himself, let him abjure his personal interests and be prepared, if need be, to accept a criminal's fate, if he wishes to follow Me.

I

With this word of Jesus the way of the disciple comes definitely into focus as the *Way of the Cross*. Let us reflect for a moment on the historical situation of Jesus and His followers at the time in question. Events had had a part in this new-shaping of the Messiah's fortunes and of the Christian calling as events must always have. The man of God cannot but relate God's will to the things that happen to him in the course of his obedience. A week or two before this time Jesus had sent the Twelve out, two by two, on their Tell-Galilee mission. They were to summon men to repentance, to deliver men from evil spirits, and to act as torch-bearers for Jesus and the Kingdom. Their mission spread the fame of Jesus, but it had also the effect of drawing upon Jesus the attention of the public authorities in Galilee. Some ominous remarks which Herod Antipas, the tetrarch of Galilee, had dropped are mentioned (Mark 6.14-16), and the Evangelist takes opportunity at this point to tell in full the story of Herod's dastardly betrayal of John the Baptist (Mark 6.14-29). It may have been also at this time, when the Twelve were absent, that an incident occurred which is recorded by St. Luke alone and at another point in the narrative. Intimation was brought to Jesus by certain Pharisees that His days in Galilee must now be regarded as numbered. Herod Antipas was moving to put Him out of the way (Luke 13.31-33). When the Twelve came back, knowing nothing of this situation, Jesus called them into quiet; they were excited over the events of their recent mission, and He said: 'Come yourselves apart, and rest awhile' (Mark 6.30-31). That a crisis had arrived is plain. It is shown by the fact that at this moment thousands of adherents of Jesus in Galilee surged round the northern end of the lake to anticipate His arrival with the Twelve at their rendezvous on the eastern shore (Mark 6.33). Why should these excited crowds set out on that expedition to the wilds if the idea had not got abroad among them that Jesus was now leaving Galilee? So we are told of the emotion displayed by Jesus at the sight: 'He had compassion on them, because they were like sheep without a shepherd' (Mark 6.34). The compassion would have special point if, as Jesus now knew, these adherents were so soon to be left without His presence and guidance. There follows the sacramental act of the Feeding of the people in the wilderness. It was our Lord's last public ministration to His Galilean followers.

We have called the Feeding in the wilderness a sacramental act. The reason for so doing is that, whatever may have been the original character of the incident, the language in which it is reported in all the accounts which have come down to us in the Gospels shows a form closely assimilated in certain features to the narrative of the Last Supper on the night before the death of Jesus. There are six accounts of the wilderness incident in the Gospels (two in Mark, two in Matthew, one in Luke and one in John), and it is difficult to determine whether the two recorded in Mark and Matthew represent different events or variant traditions of one and the same event. Be that as it may, in all cases a definite liturgical stamp has been given to the act of Jesus in the blessing and distribution of the loaves and the fishes. Jesus looks up to heaven, blesses and breaks the bread and the other viands, and gives them to the disciples to distribute to the multitudes. The solemn form of blessing and breaking bread was, indeed, the habitual and familiar overture to all religious meals among the Jews. Either, therefore, we may suppose that the tradition of the act current in the Church fastened on this feature of the incident and by its particular emphasis gave the Feeding an aspect assimilating it definitively to the later sacramental act of the Last Supper as commemorated in the Breaking of Bread in the Church; or we may regard the act of Jesus as from the start sacramental in its intention, as being indeed an actual anticipation in some sense of what He was to do at the Last Supper, and consider that this aspect of the incident has been preserved, despite the temptation in popular circles in the Church to magnify and develop the merely physical character of the event as an act of power. Upon either view the act has a special significance and stands in close relation to the shadow of rejection and suffering which had by this time gathered around the head of Jesus.

This now helps to explain the intimation to the Twelve about the denying of self and the acceptance of a life of sacrifice. It comes after the confession of St. Peter at Caesarea Philippi (Mark 8.27-28). At

Caesarea the apostle had declared his Master to be the Christ of God, still understanding by the Christ the national Messiah. It is not strange that the re-action of Jesus at that moment should be to forbid His followers the use in public of such Messianic language (Mark 8.29). He had not sought national estimation or repute, and it was plain at this crisis in His history that no national glory was to be accepted, even if He had wished it. He had been warned out of Galilee. He was a proscribed man. So comes a new departure in His teaching marked definitely at this point by the appearance and consistent use in St. Mark's record of the term *Son of Man* to indicate the office and function of Jesus. 'He began to teach them that the Son of Man must suffer much and be rejected' (Mark 8.31 f.). The Son of Man was the representative or guardian of Israel who, according to the prophetic vision in Daniel 7.13 f., was to receive an everlasting kingdom; but the mark of this kingdom was that it was to be *not from man but from God*. So it is not strange that the changed aspect now assumed by the fortunes of Jesus should reflect itself in the new turn given to the calling of His followers. They too were to accept a destiny governed not by human choices but by the will of God. In this sense they too were to come to the world of men not as from men but from God. In their original signi-ficance the words about denying themselves and taking up the cross meant for the Twelve the very literal sacrifice of their homes and kindred and possessions in Galilee, and the taking of their lives in their hands in order to go with their Master to Jerusalem. Jesus said that for them to follow Him from this time onwards was as much as their lives were worth. But the words had a larger sense and application which have now to be considered.

2

The Evangelists—or at least two of them—at this point say a very remarkable thing. Sometimes in reading the Gospels we have difficulty in making out what part of the recorded teaching of our Lord, apart from His parables, was intended for general hearers and what part was intended for the inner circle of the apostles. But here there is the definitive statement that Jesus' word about cross-bearing was universal in its application. St. Mark says He called the 'multitude' to Him along with His disciples (Mark 8.34), and St. Luke says He spoke the saying to 'all' as well as to the Twelve (Luke 9.23; cf. also 14.25-33). This must never be forgotten. The word about negating self and shouldering a cross was not understood by the tradition underlying the Gospels as a word directed to apostles only or to a special class of followers in a particular situation. It is lodged at heart of the common Christian calling. Despite our Lord's sympathy with nature and His interest in the whole ordinary life of men, He here plants the Cross between His followers and the generality of mankind, so that the *Overcoming of Self* becomes the critical issue in the working out of Christian life and destiny. Man's proper life can only come by his dying to himself.

Let it be looked at in this way. In the first stage of their following of the Christ it might appear as if all the new knowledge of God and life gained by the disciples was only an upper storey built upon the foundation of their natural lives, only an extra finish or veneer administered to their culture but leaving the original instincts of their souls untouched. But now, with the striking in of the existential note 'Say No to thyself! Negate thyself!' there comes an end to this idea. The life which the Christian is called to live with Christ is not simply an improved version or expansion of the life he has lived in the past. It shows itself as the *contradiction* of that former life!

We may say that for the Christian in the school of Christ the life he is called upon to live will now, sooner or later, and certainly in every situation of true self-understanding or external crisis, shape itself as the opposite of the life he has been or is now living. Negate thy *self*! That word means that the disciple must forever tell himself that the truly Christian life is the life he has not got, and that he must daily be prepared to be made over differently if he is to continue as a follower of Christ. In such a situation we discern more closely the meaning of the word addressed by Jesus to Nicodemus in the Fourth Gospel about the necessity of the spiritual birth 'from above' (John 3.3,5), which means a new existence; it is the Kingdom of God saying No to our original nature and self-satisfied living. It is also to be remembered that, in the call to self-negation, self includes not only our personal spirit but the material world in its hold upon our spirit. The world is too much with us. It tends to enslave us. It makes our interests ego-centric. And 'what does it profit a man if he gains the whole world and forfeits his life?'

Let there be no misunderstanding about this

matter. Jesus was not speaking of higher or lower values or levels of life in any general sense. He was speaking of the coming of the *Kingdom of God* at the earliest moment as the one critical issue of life. He was making entrance into that Kingdom the goal and test of life. To share in that Kingdom was to go with Him to Jerusalem at whatever cost of present interest and security. Nevertheless, the demand has relation to man's true life under any conceivable set of conditions, and thus it has continued to lay its imperative on the Church. It continued to do so after the hope of the Return of Christ as an immediate or early historical event ceased to dominate the Christian mind, and Christians had to adjust their thoughts to a continuance of historical life in the world.

The principle then was, and remains, that it is not through simple improvement or increase in knowledge or ethical insight that the way of the Christian disciple lies, but through *obedience*, commitment, surrender, the taking of the yoke of Jesus. Yet the negation of self which is thus demanded is not, rightly understood, the renunciation of nature so much as the renunciation of the selfish or self-first principle which has entered into nature, and which in human nature means that a man not only clings to what is less than his proper life, but holds back, hesitates, fears and evades that proper life when it is offered to him. All these things—reserve, fear, hesitation and evasion—come under the ban of the Say-no-to-thyself principle. Nor does the way out of the impasse lie merely in ascetic measures of discipline, the renouncing of things, for such renunciation may be only another form of retreat into the Ego, another device of the self-defence mechanism by which a man thinks to direct his life to higher things while still keeping the regulation of it in his own hands. Jesus Christ does not strike at things but at Self, and self-righteousness is only a form of the ego-assertive consciousness. Rather is the way to be sought in a displacement of the personal centre of interest, in an outgoing of our life to Christ and a fuller sharing with Him in the spirit of His love and passion. Negating the self means, in effect, letting the *Christ* replace our own Ego as the actuating principle of life in us, so that our life shall become His life in us, the expression in us of His mind, love and will, so that it shall carry with it the emergence in us of a new personality, a character determined not by self-will but by the spirit of the Son of Man.

3

What the conditions and the character of that new life are to be in the period between the earthly life of Jesus and His Coming in glory to fulfil the promise of the Kingdom will still need to be considered. We shall be concerned with that question in our next study. But to the central principle of that life— Christ fulfilling Himself in the Christian, men being constrained in Him to rise on stepping-stones of their dead selves to higher things—to that central principle the New Testament bears witness on every page.

Not first that which is spiritual, but that which is natural; afterwards that which is spiritual (I Cor. 15.46).

So writes St. Paul, contrasting Adam and Christ, the head of the old humanity and the head of the new, the principle of human self-centredness on the one hand and the principle of love outgoing to God on the other. There is no doubting which of these principles is prior in the chronology and history of the human race. Whatever idealists may say, Adam started us off. But in the Gospel there is the promise of a higher life supervening—'afterwards that which is spiritual'. So the Apostle goes on to say:

> And as we have borne the image of the earthly, we shall also bear the image of the heavenly (I Cor. 15.49).

Between the two, however, between life according to nature and life according to grace, there stands the Cross!

.   .   .   .   .

May I conclude these reflections with an apologue?

In the county of Northumberland, close to Warkworth Castle, a meadow slopes down from the Castle to the River Coquet. You walk down the meadow and come to the brink of the river. A winding path conducts you down the wooded side of a deep gorge, and at the foot is a small landing-stage on the water. A ferryman and his boat come alongside. You step aboard, and with a few strokes of the oar the ferryman takes you upstream to another landing-stage with a flight of steps ascending the sheer face of a cliff. And there at the top is a little oratory carved out of the solid rock in the form of a Gothic vault.

It was made for prayer, this vault, in the long-ago. By whom? and why? We have no knowledge. Perhaps a monk from a nearby monastery carved it out for a hermitage. But interpretation is free, and perhaps it was some man of blood who had repented of his sins and had turned to religion who built this shrine for his soul's peace with God. If so, we may think of words like these as passing through his mind and keeping company with the strokes of his mallet and chisel:

> Have mercy upon me, O God, according to Thy
> loving kindness;
> According to the multitude of Thy tender mercies
> blot out my transgressions.
> Wash me. . . . Cleanse me from my sin!
> For I acknowledge my transgressions
> and my sin is ever before me.

The prayer for a new heart would be there, and for the restoration of the joy of God's salvation:

> My sacrifice, O God, is a broken spirit; a broken and
> contrite heart, O God, Thou wilt not despise.

And then, it may be, there would come into his mind the tremendous lapidary words of the Apostle to the Gentiles:

> The first man is of the earth, earthy; the second man
> is from heaven.

> As is the earthy, so also are those that are earthy, and
> as is the heavenly, so also are those that are heavenly.

> And as we have borne the image of the earthy, we
> shall also bear the image of the heavenly.

That, at any rate, is the kind of change which in the course of the disciples' walk with Christ becomes proposed to the Christian.

PRAYER

LORD JESUS CHRIST, *who didst tread the path of obedience for our sakes, and when men turned from Thee, didst give Thyself to die upon the Cross for our sins; grant that we may hear Thy voice, and take up our cross and follow Thee, that through the fellowship of Thine obedience we may know the deathless power of Thy victory over the world; for Thy name's sake.* Amen.

IV

SACRAMENTAL LIFE

And when the hour was come, He sat down, and the apostles with Him. And He said unto them, With desire I have desired to eat this Passover with you before I suffer.
St. Luke 22.14

And as they were eating, He took bread, and when He had blessed, He brake it, and gave to them, and said, Take ye: this is My body. And He took a cup, and when He had given thanks, He gave to them: and they all drank of it. And He said unto them, This is My blood of the covenant which is shed for many. Verily I say unto you, I will no more drink of the fruit of the vine, until that day when I drink it new in the kingdom of God.
St. Mark 14.22-25

WE must now pass to a third stage in the unfolding of the Christian way of life. It is the stage indicated by the special event of Thursday in Holy Week, on which day our Lord instituted the solemn rite of the Sacrament of His Body and Blood. In what relation does this supreme act of grace stand to the character and completeness of the Christian life? What is its meaning and function with reference to that life?

I

We have followed the initial stages in the formation of the Christian way of life: first the entrance into discipline-fellowship with Jesus Christ on life's road, and secondly, the call of disciples to the overcoming of self. In our last meditation we came to see that, faced by the requirement to deny himself, the

E

follower of Jesus is brought to the realization that the Christian life is not a life which he has got in himself, or can regard as an achieved possession, since he has to *negate* himself in order to find it. The life of discipleship stands, in fact, at every point in contradiction to his natural way of living. The man who comes to Christ is asked to seek *God's* reign and righteousness (Matt. 6.33). He is confronted with the Sermon on the Mount with its demands of purity, truth, humility, trust and love, and he is told that he must stroke out his own Ego if he is to remain a follower of the Son of Man.

At this point two things will have become reasonably plain to him: first, the inconceivableness that God's will for him should ever be less absolute and exacting than Jesus has declared it to be, and secondly, the impossibility of his attaining in himself to that perfection of obedience which Jesus has asked. But what now if the consciousness thus present at the beginning of his Christian existence should go on attending him all the way? What if he must continue all the time saying to himself in the words made familiar by St. Paul: 'To will (the good) is present with me, but how to perform that which is good is not' (Rom. 7.18)? Where in that case is the *completeness* of the Christian life to be looked for?

The meaning of the famous seventh chapter of Romans is not always properly understood. Ordinarily the soul-despair to which the chapter gives utterance is referred to a stage in the Apostle's spiritual history before Christ and His grace came into his life. This was the view taken by the early Greek Fathers, such as Origen, and it has come to be widely accepted by many people in modern times. Over against this view stands, however, the difficulty of locating a time in the Apostle's *Jewish* life when he was, as he says (Rom. 7.9), 'without the Law', i.e. not touched or affected by that Law, not coming within the scope of the Law and, still more, the difficulty of understanding how as a Jew he could come to that despair of the Law which the chapter seems to describe. As a practising Jew Saul of Tarsus, if he felt his own obedience to the law of God to be defective, would say with his Jewish contemporaries: Well, let me pray more, and fast more, and give myself to more and better study of the sacred books! No Jew as sincere as the man of Tarsus could, through any experience short of a higher revelation from God than the Law, come to question the Law as the divinely appointed way of salvation, or think that from the Law the glory and grace of God had departed. Consequently other interpreters, including St. Augustine and the Western Fathers, and the Reformers, especially John Calvin, have taken the chapter as the description of some aspect or mood of St. Paul's *Christian* experience. They call attention to the fact that the 'will' of which the chapter speaks is good and consents to the Law of God (Rom. 7.21-22) and that the source of Paul's trouble is that the power to achieve complete obedience to that Law is absent. This would seem to point in the right direction at least for an answer to the real problem of the chapter. St. Paul is not, indeed, giving a full-orbed account of the Christian experience in Romans 7. For that we must turn over the page to Romans 8.

But he is obliged for the moment to deal with the position of Christians in the Church—compare Romans 6.15 and Galatians 3.1-5—who, doubtful of the adequacy of St. Paul's sole reliance on grace, apparently insisted or assumed that the Law had value *in itself* as contributing to the completeness of the Christian salvation. This assumption the Apostle denies as not founded upon fact. By a dialectical analysis of the state of the soul faced by the imperative of righteousness he shows that the goodness and holiness of the Law may be fully acknowledged while the power to render a sufficient obedience is not present. And this brings us back to the question: Where, in that case, is the completeness of the Christian life to be sought?

2

This is a question which concerns not only the Christian in his individual existence. It concerns the whole Church in respect of its social task and responsibility. In a volume of theological essays published a few years ago under the title of *The Christian Answer* (1946), there is a chapter on 'Christianity and the Christian' in which Dr. John Knox of New York pays some attention to the point. This author has a keen sense of the dilemma—to which modern poetry as well as theology bears ample witness—into which Christian people are thrown through their being conscious, on the one hand, of the perfect Will of God as regards their personal and public duty and, on the other hand, of their inability to find in themselves the knowledge and power to carry that Will through. For example, there is the difficulty which we find in reconciling 'our relatively comfortable way of life' with 'the enormity of human need about us'. Yet who, he asks, is clear as to what should and can be done in the situation? Jesus has defined the Will of God in unmistakable terms: Give your all, love your enemies, withhold help from no one, forget yourself—and no lesser terms can ever satisfy us as corresponding to the measure of our Christian duty. Yet, to use St. Paul's language again, we are only too conscious of another law in our nature militating against the divine principle which our minds acknowledge as right, and holding us captives under the power of our natural sinfulness (Rom. 7.23), and this reduces us, to say the least of it, to a sense of continuous incompleteness.

Yes! God does not dilute His righteousness. He does not say that something less than His own perfection will suffice as our norm of life (Matt. 5.48). He does not negotiate with us on the level of our human possibilities. How, then, do the grace and the gospel of Jesus Christ enter into the situation? We are called to consecration, yet the attainment of it on the human side is not thinkable. The writer I have quoted puts the conclusion of the matter thus:

> We are incapable, simply in virtue of our being human, of perfect obedience to the demands of love. . . . We cannot define our obligation short of bearing the sins of the world, but it is not within our power even to bear our own. Only God can carry so intolerable a load. That He does so is the meaning of the Cross.

Only God can carry a load like that, the load of our duty, the load of our responsibility, the load of the obligation of love which we owe to one another! Is it not here that we begin to see the way out, the solution of the dilemma, so far as the true nature of our Christian calling is concerned? The life we are called to live is *the life of God in us*. It must therefore be the act of God in us enabling us to bear the burden which we face. It must be God's righteousness made available for us. A little earlier, when we were considering our Lord's word about repentance, we saw that, while Jesus Christ calls all His followers to turn towards God and while this turning is essential, no man can of himself fill in the fulness of that God-surrendered life. No man can give himself a new mentality, a new nature, a new heart, nor did Jesus teach that we could. Jesus did not say that men achieve the full conversion of themselves. Their primary concern in this matter was with *God*. Their part was to give themselves to God, to abandon themselves to the God whose will it was to bring in His Kingdom. So now with regard to Christian righteousness. The righteousness of the Kingdom is God's righteousness, not ours (Matt. 6.33; cf. 5.48), and therefore the fulness of the Christian life is something for which we are dependent on God, which therefore must be put our way by God. It is for us to place ourselves in God's hands; it is for Him to work in us both will and deed on behalf of His purpose. Given the penitent spirit on our side, the sincere intention, and a heart open to God, a start at least is made and the divine purpose can be trusted to go forwards: 'Faithfulness will spring from the ground, and righteousness will look down from heaven. Yea, the Lord will give what is good' (Psalm

85.11). Moreover, the divine intention includes within the scope of its operation not only the life that now is but the life hereafter.

3

Now here, surely, we see the relation in which the *Sacrament* stands to the wholeness of the Christian life. What the Sacrament signifies is that God in Christ bridges the gulf, closes the gap between our Christian incompleteness and Himself. The fulness of the Christian life depends in the end on God. The followers of Jesus are called to *Sacramental Life*.

Up to this point, as we will remember, Jesus and His disciples had been travelling as a team. But the time was to come when He was to draw apart from the company, to put a distance between Himself and them, and to go forward to a single and indivisible destiny. Even at a point on the journey up to Jerusalem we read that 'Jesus was going before them, and they were amazed, and they that followed were afraid' (Mark 10.32). The actual separation was not yet, but the act of Jesus was significant and premonitory. We also find the members of the company divided by personal ambitions and wrangling about the priorities and privileges which would be theirs when their Master came into His Kingdom. Jesus was to say to these men very soon: 'You will all be scandalized, for it is written, I will smite the shepherd, and the sheep shall be scattered abroad' (Mark 14.27). In the Garden of Gethsemane even the most intimate three of the disciple-group were to be spectators only of His passion, not participants. At His arrest they were to forsake Him, and at

Calvary where were they to be? Lost in the crowd, if not with those who were alienated from Him, at least with those who wrung the hands, who knew that somehow they were implicated in the tragedy of Golgotha, but could do nothing about it!

In that last hour there was not to be a single one of the disciples over whose sense of his relation to Jesus there was not to steal the consciousness that, despite all the knowledge and grace he had gained in the school of Christ, his indecision or cowardice or weakness had some part in that 'fearful enmity of the carnal heart of man towards God' which raged round Jesus in the trial-hall and at the cross. The position of Judas we know. But of the others there was not to be one whose moral conscience was not to assail him in that existential hour. So this is the position into which, so far as the Twelve were concerned, the gracious calling of the Lord was to bring them before the day was done; standing afar off from Jesus, discovered to themselves, and in effect saying. as all in such judgement-hours must say:

> My sins have taken such an hold on me,
> I am not able to look up to Thee;
> Lord, I repent; accept my tears and grief!

But before this separation and this discovery what is it that Jesus, having loved His own which were in the world and still loving them to the end, does to prepare them for the self-accusing depth of awakened conscience into which His death is going to plunge them? What step does He take to confirm and to secure the permanence of that communion with Himself into which His now shaken followers had at His calling entered for the sake of the Kingdom of God? How does He act so as to bind these men for ever to Himself, and to give to His solitary sacrifice so positive and inclusive a relation to their lives that its fulness will cover all their incompleteness? There are some who think, without sacramental aids or assurances of any kind, to be able, in the sole strength of an unassisted spiritual apprehension, to bear the full weight of the moral self-discovery which is inseparable from the Christian life. Such an attitude forgets the part which effectual signs from God have played in all ages in the history of Biblical religion, and above all it overlooks the infinite depths of the necessity and mercy in which the Saviour, on the night on which He was betrayed, acted towards those so-soon-to-be-broken-and-discredited men whom He had gathered around Him, and whom, all but one, He had kept. Jesus was dealing with disciples to whom the *Word* had come, who had learned much about God and about their heavenly calling, but who had also come to know *themselves*, who were shaken to the depths by that discovery, and who knew themselves unclean, condemned and powerless apart from Him.

But *Vexilla Regis Prodeunt*! The words of the ancient Latin hymn, 'The Royal Banners Forward Go', come to us as having a special bearing on the Saviour's act at this great moment.

At a certain point in the course of the meal Jesus took a loaf of bread and, having blessed, He broke and gave it to them, saying: 'Take, this is My body'. The meaning is: 'This, the thing proferred, is I

Myself, My person, My life, which is being given
for you. Take Me to yourselves.' He took also a cup
and after thanksgiving gave it to them to drink, with
the words: 'This is My blood of the Covenant, which
is poured out for many'. The words 'Blood of the
Covenant' recall the terms of the first covenant made
by God with Israel, which was sealed by sacrifice
(Exod. 24.8). Since then, a New Covenant had been
promised (Jer. 31.31 ff.), and with the words 'My
blood of the Covenant' Jesus is sealing by the
sacrifice of His life that *New Covenant* of grace.

4

Such in simple outline is the institution, the special
event of Thursday in Holy Week. It was observed
on an earlier occasion that all Christian repentance
has to be interpreted as God working in us. Now we
see all Christian life as God's action for us and in us,
coming as it does under the sign of the Sacrament,
the broken body and shed blood of Christ. Jesus had
said 'Follow Me!' He had said 'Deny thyself!' Now
He says 'Take, this is My Body!' He is by this act
bridging the gulf, closing the gap between Himself
and us, between our guilt and powerlessness and His
own perfect offering of His life to God. In a brief
meditation it is not possible to dwell on all the aspects
of the *Effectual Sign* given by the Sacrament, but this
may be said. (1) Under one of its aspects the Lord's
Supper is an anticipation of the coming again of
Christ in glory and of His re-union with His
followers. Under the circumstances of the immediate
moment—in which the Shepherd is about to be
smitten, and the sheep about to be scattered—Jesus

speaks of the Messianic banquet in the fulfilled Kingdom of God, and says to His followers that He and they will meet again. This is with reference to their impending *separation* from Him. Jesus is over-arching this separation with the pledge to His followers of their continuing communion and one-ness with Himself.

But (2) there is another aspect. The New Testament witness to the Sacrament instituted by our Lord in the Upper Room does not leave us only with its forward-pointing significance as an anticipation of the Messianic banquet in the Coming Kingdom and of the re-union of the faithful there. According to the narratives of the institution both in I Corinthians 11 and in Mark 14 (and the parallel Synoptic narratives), Jesus has wrought something for us now which marks the transmission to us of the redeeming effects of His sacrifice. The Bread and the Cup are not only exhibited, but *given*. If our Lord, holding out the Bread, and raising in His hands the Cup, had only pointed to those objects, saying 'This is My body' and 'This is My blood of the Covenant', the Sacrament, however undyingly impressive in its form, would have remained only a sign or demon-stration of His vicarious sacrifice, and thus would convey at best a lesson to be laid to our hearts. But as the Elements are given with the command 'Take ye', 'Drink ye', the Sacrament has to do not only with the coming separation of the Lord and His disciples, but with the disciples' sense of present *guilt, insufficiency and powerlessness*, which the Lord overcomes by this final proof of His complete identification of Himself with them. His sacrifice is being made on their behalf. It covers and includes them. Its substance is communicated to them. They are taken into union with His perfect offered life. They are made beneficiaries of His obedience. Their guilt is taken over by Him and atoned for. Their incompleteness is swallowed up in Him. Thus to their lives there is given the character to which St. Paul bears witness when he represents, as the logic of the whole Christian position, this: 'I have been crucified with Christ, and it is no longer I who live, but Christ lives in me; and the life I now live in the flesh I live by faith in the Son of God, who loved me and gave Himself for me' (Gal. 2.19-20). There at last the Christian life is defined in its *completeness*.

In St. Paul's description of the Christian life as life 'in Christ', the Apostle is indicating his complete acceptance of the position asserted in his word (II Cor. 5.14): 'One died for all, therefore all died; and He died for all, that they which live should no longer live unto themselves, but unto Him who for their sakes died and rose again.' As he works out the great thought of the Saviour's self-identification with us in life and death, it is made plain that Christ is at once (1) the ground of the life of faith, and (2) the sphere or milieu within which that life of faith is lived. At the same time, as the Sacrament shows, Christ is (3) the substance of our life, that on which it feeds, and (4) He is the goal or end of our life, for the Sacrament is 'until He *comes*' (I Cor. 11.26). The gifts also which are offered to us in the Pauline gospel are gifts of the ascended and glorified Redeemer, gifts in which He Himself is imparted: Righteousness, Sonship to God, the Holy Spirit, Victory and Peace.

Therefore it is that all Christian life attains its finality only under the sign of the Sacrament. In our Baptism we are taken into a share in the holy, once-for-all baptism of Jesus, and in the Lord's Supper we are made partakers of the final giving of His life in our stead. Should not the thought of sacramental life be so extended as to apply in a real way to all spheres of human activity? We have referred once or twice to the very real interest which the Church has in bringing these activities—science, art, industry, politics, education, commerce—into relation with the gospel. If Jesus Christ is the incarnation of the Eternal Word by which the world was made, then His teaching and His significance lie not away from the world, but have an organic bearing on its life. The demands which scientific and technological developments are making on us today are so clamorous and inordinate as to seem to threaten the whole place of religion in our midst. Must not this danger be countered and this fear dispelled by the Church courageously re-asserting that all these spheres of activity come under the sovereignty and under the sacrifice of the Christian Mediator? The gospel of the redeeming love of God is organic to all life, not only in point of its ethic of love and obedience, but in point of its sacramental promise of completeness. All life should be claimed as potentially sacramental, as called to understand itself in the light of the sacrificial offering of Christ. The Church should take not only its gospel into the market place and the factory, but its Holy Table, saying to all the world's workers: 'Come, take by faith the body of your Lord!'

PRAYER

Lord Jesus Christ, who, departing to the Father, didst leave with Thy disciples the assurance that they belonged to Thee, and would share with Thee in the glory of Thy Kingdom; Grant us, for the sake of the same hope, to live a pure and holy life, walking in Thy footsteps, and believing that Thou hereafter wilt remove from us the taint and stain of sin, and bestow on us the holiness of perfection; for Thy love's sake. Amen.

V

O ALL-ATONING SACRIFICE!

God was in Christ, reconciling the world unto Himself, not reckoning unto them their trespasses. . . . Him who knew no sin He made to be sin on our behalf: that we might become the righteousness of God in Him.   II Cor. 5.19,21

I

WE pass to the last event of Holy Week, the act in which the New Testament sees the culmination-point of the Manifestation of God in Christ. God the Father, in order to win the world back to Himself and to forgive us our sins, puts the sinless Christ in our stead, identifying the Obedient Son with the mass of the world's transgression, and for Christ's sake He accepts forgiven sinners as the body of those in whom He is well pleased (II Cor. 5.21). Such is the amazing paradox which the apostolic gospel of the New Testament sets before us. It is a conception which upsets human accounts, overturns human standards, and contradicts human assumptions—for where in all the world had the salvation of God been thought of as coming about in a form like this? But there are points—and this is one of them—at which the human mind has been led to find its highest wisdom and exercise in suspending human judgements and leaving room for God to be God. Christianity has so acted. It has found a reasonable basis for its faith, and in the paradox of the Cross has seen the power and the wisdom of God. Whereas

Jews, argues St. Paul, ask for 'signs' and Greeks seek after 'wisdom', we preach a crucified Christ, who shocks the Jews and is a subject for raillery among the Greeks, but who to those who are called, whether Jews or Greeks, is the power and the wisdom of God (I Cor. 1.22-24). That is to say, while Jews ask for external miracles of power, and Greeks demand a rational understanding of the universe, we Christians look upon the Crucified Christ as God's supreme miracle, and at the same time we see in Him God's way of answering all our questions.

Here indeed *is* the focal point at which, for Christian faith, God and man come together. And it is not strange that when they come together it should be after the pattern of the Cross on which the Son of Man is stretched. The conception that the truly righteous man, whose life was governed by the pure love of virtue and not by consideration of any of its rewards, would be tortured and impaled by unrighteous society was familiar enough to the ancient world. There is a famous statement to that effect in the argument which is placed on the lips of Glauco in a celebrated passage of Plato (*Republic*, II, 361E). But in the New Testament it is not the righteous man and immoral society that confront each other in Jesus, but the love of God and the sin of the world!

> O love of God! O sin of man!
> In this dread act your strength is tried,
> And victory remains with love!

Scripture had taught that God's thoughts are not our thoughts, and His ways are not our ways. At this

point, therefore, we who have followed the steps of
the first disciples in their earthly walk with the Son
of Man must, like these disciples, stand aside, that
God may do His strange work. The *It is finished* of
this transaction is the Lord's work, not man's.
Mystery, deep as the terrestrial darkness which
covers Golgotha from noon to three, wraps itself
around the Crucified, and there is a silence unbroken,
according to our earliest Gospel, except by a single
cry. Yet as we stand there, looking at the Cross,
certain things come into clearness. Only a *love* like
that of Jesus, who came to make Himself one with
sinners that He might bring sinners to God, explains
His fate and sets its purpose in the right perspective.
He came not to be ministered unto, but to minister
and to give His life a ransom for many (Mark 10.45).
So the Christian teaching in its earliest pronounce-
ments on the subject can say: 'Christ died for our
sins' (I Cor. 15.3), or as the First Epistle of Peter
puts it: 'He died, the Just for the Unjust, that He
might bring you to God' (3.18).

2

Let us look more closely at the mystery of Calvary.
What we see, first, is the *portentous massing of human
evil* against the person of Jesus in His life and in
His death. Jesus is fated from the beginning to draw
upon Himself the sins of men in their worst and most
malignant forms. From the moment of His baptism,
when first He associated Himself with sinners at the
river Jordan and heard the divine voice say to Him

F

'Thou art my Son, in Thee I am well pleased', the powers of evil are alerted against Him. The words 'Thou art my Son', in which the New Testament theology has come to see the declaration of God's purpose to undo the work of Satan by the setting forward of His obedient Servant Jesus as the elect head of a new humanity, is the signal to the demonic forces in the world to concert their united powers against Him. In the wilderness Satan tries to pluck the Kingdom of God out of the hands of the obedient Son. In Galilee Jesus flings Himself into the battle for the souls of men against the same adversary and against his minions who have possessed and crazed the minds of men, but when He intervenes to save these sufferers and to restore their souls to God, the spirits round on Him and say: 'What have we to do with Thee Jesus of Nazareth? Hast Thou come to destroy us?' It is war *à outrance* with the spiritual powers. The religious opponents of Jesus, the scribes and Pharisees, are not slow to make capital out of the engagement of Jesus to deliver these souls, and are found plotting with the sycophants of Herod Antipas to put Him out of the way. Later, Jesus is found saying: 'From the days of John the Baptist [that is, from the time of Jesus' own baptism] until now, the kingdom of heaven is violently assaulted and the violent are seeking to wrest it to themselves (Matt. 11.12). While this enigmatic word has perplexed interpreters, and appears in a greatly softened form in the parallel passage in Luke 16.16, there can be little doubt as to its original force. Jesus is saying that from the moment, when the heavenly voice made known to Him His destiny as the

Messiah-Son of God, malignant evil has reared its head against Him, thwarting, opposing and traducing Him because He proclaims God's will to deliver and save lost men.

So Jesus is set from the beginning to draw the sin of the world towards and upon Himself, and He knows that this situation must be accepted as the condition and the price of finishing His work. 'I came,' He said, 'to cast fire upon the earth, and how I would it were already kindled! But I have a baptism to be baptized with, and how constrained I am until it is accomplished!' (Luke 12.49-50). The 'fire' of which He spoke must in its connection with His 'baptism' refer to the fire of judgement which, according to John the Baptist's prediction, the Coming One, the Deliverer, was to apply to human society (Luke 3.16-17; Matt. 3.10-12). Jesus knows that this fire is not *yet* kindled. His baptism has not *yet* been completed. Something stands in the way, nor can there be any doubt as to the nature of the resistance which is meant. The enmity of *sin* still interposes itself between mankind and God's coming to reign. Pass on now to the closing spectacle of the drama in which the Saviour is arraigned before His accusers in the trial-hall. All the world's worst is come upon Him and is loaded in accusation against Him. There is Caiaphas, head of the priesthood, chief of those ministers of religion who have received the law and the sacred oracles, the Urim and Thummim, to give to Israel. How does Caiaphas appear at this moment? As cynical head of a political party, that will callously extirpate the leader of a potentially dangerous Messianic movement in order not to risk a breach with the Roman authority! There are the Pharisees, the holiness party among the Jews, sanctimonious to a degree, and scrupulous for righteousness. But they have accused Jesus of blasphemy because of the personal authority which He claims to interpret the law and the tradition, and they have already proscribed Him as confederate with the powers of darkness. There is the Roman soldiery, set to act as guardians of the peace, but now venting on Jesus their sadistic malevolence against the Jews. There is Pilate, the man in authority, who despises the Jews, the priests and the truth. What is Pilate doing? Abandoning his innocent prisoner to His enemies on an unproved charge, and washing his magisterial hands of all responsibility in the matter. And there is the crowd that wants Barabbas. All forms of human iniquity have come together to point their arrows at the heart of Jesus. He must representatively draw the world's worst upon Himself, 'the whole fearful enmity of the carnal heart of man towards God', and not only must He face it. He must take all the guilt and penalty of it upon Himself.

For here in all this hatred and cynicism and corruption in religion and politics is the sign of God's judgement on sin. God's judgement on sin comes out in the malignant course which evil in the heart of man goes on proposing and re-proposing to itself, and this malignancy is now directed and concentrated against Jesus Christ. Was there no way out, no way of escape for the obedient Son? An hour or two before, in the Garden of Gethsemane, Jesus had prayed to the Father that, if it was His will, the hour might pass from Him. So much depended on the issue of that dread hour! If death was to be the portion of Jesus, might it not mean the extinction of the faith of His followers and the end of all the work He had striven on earth to do? The ordeal was a very intense one. 'Being on the Mount of Olives,' writes Dr. Lowrie in his *Jesus According to St. Mark*, 'Jesus was already on the road to Galilee—how easy to follow (that road) with the full moon of the Passover night!' But, No! Jesus had come as the obedient Son to bring Israel to God and forgiveness, and He must see the work through. He must do the will of Him who had sent Him and finish His work. But if that was to be done, if the many whom He had grasped in His saving hand were not to be abandoned, Jesus must experience the whole brunt, the full equivalent of all this 'fearful enmity of the carnal heart of man towards God', and accept the Cross to which it pointed. His resolution to do so was His taking on Him of the sin of the world. Jesus becomes by this act 'the body of sin', that He may say of His work: 'It is finished!'

3

But if we see in the Cross the magnitude of human evil, we see also, secondly, the transcendent wonder of the *Divine forgiveness*. He who accepts the Cross does so in the spirit of 'Father, forgive them, for they know not what they do.' Face to face with the event on Calvary, we have to give ourselves account finally of what is involved in real forgiveness. What can take away our *sin*? Sometimes we speak as if all that is needed for deliverance from sin is repentance towards God. But can repentance, can even remorse ever of itself abolish the guilt and curse of sin? We may say that the Bible promises forgiveness to those who are penitent, and so it does. But that is because in the Bible *God* takes over and deals with the sin. All forgiveness exercised by men is but the reflection of, the faint derivative of the supreme act of God, but what does the act of God mean? In the Old Testament sin is cancelled, and communion with God re-established only by rites of atoning sacrifice which God provides and which remove the barrier between the sinner and Himself. God forgives the repentant because He *translates* their guilt away from them: their sin is covered, their iniquity is removed. In the New Testament also guilt is removed by being translated. But translated where?

For fifty years we have been told that the modern man is not troubling about his sins nor about the problem of their pardon. It does not appear what title the merely being modern gives a man to exempt himself from the fatality and the curse which— witness the great tragedians from Aeschylus and Sophocles onwards—hang over moral evil and guilt in the world. It is quite certain that no normal man whose eyes are at all open to the facts of his moral history can look with equanimity on the record unless he is past feeling: acts he has done which he can never more undo, words he has spoken which he can never more take back, opportunities he has lost and can never more retrieve, amends he has not made and can never more repair! When we think of the part played in the normal broken count of life by cruelty, ingratitude, selfishness, insincerity, indolence, envy and broken faith, can we think that repentance itself is enough to dispose of the *objective evil* that has been wrought? But what can clear that objective evil away or obliterate that guilt? Can a man go to *nature* and expect a bill of clearance? Nature never forgets or forgives, she does not cancel a breach of her laws. Can we go to other *men* to ask for a quiet conscience? Our friends will be sympathetic, they will forgive our wrongs against them, but, as the Psalmist says, 'None can by any means redeem his brother, nor give to God a ransom for him' (Psalm 49.7). These forgiving human friends have burdens enough of their own to carry without charging themselves with the full weight of ours as well. They cannot take the burden of our guilt upon their souls; they cannot, in any case, undo the effects of our transgression. Can a man, then, forgive *himself*? That is the one thing he cannot do if his conscience is alive. He may repent, but he cannot extirpate the evil he has done. Where, then, can such sin be undone, not only forgiven but blotted out? There is but one answer: it can be undone only in the heart of *God*, only by its being taken in its whole magnitude, judged, and accepted in its full equivalence, as it can be only by God *suffering* for it. Only in the heart of God at last can the sin be taken, so as not only to be borne and forgiven, but extinguished. Only the holy love of God can burn the sin to ashes, so that it is no more! In this connection are any words of Holy Scripture more affecting than those with which the prediction of the New Covenant in Jeremiah is concluded: 'I will forgive their

iniquity, and their sin I will remember no more'?
(Jer. 31.34).

4

This redeeming love of God is what the Christian
Church sees brought to light in the Passion and
Death of Jesus Christ. The obedient Son identifies
Himself here in a single act both with the Holy God
and with sinful men, and in such a way that God
and man are brought together in His body and
reconciled. Henceforth, from the Christian stand-
point, all repentance of man towards God means
acknowledgement of our sin as sin against the blood
and righteousness of Jesus Christ and acceptance of
Him as our Representative and Advocate with God.
He covers us, even to the point of accepting for our
sake the last agony of abandonment by God. Until
now, we have not mentioned our Lord's cry of
Dereliction on the Cross. While later Gospels record
other utterances of the Crucified in His dying hours,
our earliest evangelist reports only the one single
cry: *Eloi, Eloi, lama sabachthani*, 'My God, My God,
why hast Thou forsaken Me?' Some have held that
these awful words, which form the opening verse of
the twenty-second Psalm, are to be taken not in
isolation but in their association with those other
words in the Psalm in which the Sufferer sounds the
note of triumph, as for example when he says 'I will
declare Thy name unto my brethren', or again, 'All
the ends of the earth will remember and turn to the
Lord . . . for the kingdom is the Lord's', or once
again, 'They shall declare Thy salvation to a people

yet to be born, that He hath done this.' But while this interpretation is offered, and while we can all agree with Dr. Lowrie that our Lord's emphasis upon the profound significance of God's personal relation to His saints precludes the possibility of our thinking that He, the Beloved Son, forsook His hope in God even when He felt forsaken, nevertheless the cry of dereliction remains the cry of dereliction. It is *the* cry from the Cross. Dr. Lowrie's statement is made in his book *Jesus According to St. Mark* (p. 547), which has already been referred to. The evangelical word he has in mind is the passage in Mark 12.26 f.: 'But as touching the dead that they are raised, have you not read in the book of Moses, in the place relating to the Bush, how God said to him: "I am the God of Abraham, and the God of Isaac, and the God of Jacob"? He is not the God of the dead, but of the living'; to which words St. Luke adds: 'for all live unto Him'. Dr. Lowrie is impressed by the passionate emphasis with which our Lord affirmed that in this passage there was contained the sure pledge of the resurrection of the dead. But while this is so, and while the certainty of the resurrection hope remains unshaken, we must never forget the unparalleled nature of the death of Jesus on the Cross. Jesus was dying there not for Himself but in the place of sinners; He was taking their guilt and death to Himself. Could He accept this last vicarious responsibility in its totality without there closing over Him in death the utterest darkness which sinful humanity can know or without there being pressed to His lips the last drop in the sinner's cup of agony, namely his sense of the extinction of all his relations with God? It could not be. Jesus must drink to the dregs the cup which the Father had given Him.

Losing God to find man, yet not really losing God, but finding Him in the very act of finding man, and bringing God and man together in Himself! Such is the transaction of Good Friday, the closing act of the drama of Holy Week, through which, with its sequel in the Resurrection of the Crucified, is inaugurated the Christian reconciliation of the world and the rise of the Christian Church. God's holiness and man's guilt, brought together on Calvary, encountering each the other in the full reality of both, and in a realm of Spirit—*Eternal Spirit* the Epistle to the Hebrews calls it (9.14)—where at last, and where alone, the opposites are recognized for what they truly are, and justice is done to both: this is the victory of God and love in Christ, and it is the sign which in the pure light of the first Easter morning stands over the new humanity. This, because the God who brought His Son from the dead and gave Him glory, who has highly exalted Him and given Him the name which is above every name that in the name of Jesus every knee shall bow, has, as Dr. T. F. Torrance says, taken the Cross of Jesus 'and made it the instrument for the healing of the nations'. Through His Cross the Saviour is still at work in history; and if His final coming in might and judgement is postponed, it is 'because He wants first to meet with every man at His Cross, there to release him from his sin and guilt, there to ask of him the love of his heart, and there to remake him as God's dear child'.[1] Indeed, it was already made known to

[1] T. F. Torrance, *When Christ Comes and Comes Again*, pp. 20 f.

the apostolic generation (Mark 13.10; cf. II Thess. 2.1-8) that the End awaits the historical fulfilment of the preaching of the gospel to all the nations. The star of the Last Advent stands over the pathway of the Church's mission to the world.

PRAYER

LORD JESUS CHRIST, *who didst choose our sadness and sorrows, taking our sins upon Thyself, that we might be redeemed through Thee; let Thy hands support us, Thine eyes pity us, Thy feet tread down every difficulty in our upward way; may we depend upon Thee as Saviour, accept Thee as our life, choose with Thy will, and dwell in Thy heart, and in the end, through Thy enabling power and Thy victory over sin and the world, be made inheritors of Thy blessed Kingdom, to the glory of Thy name, who with the Father and the Holy Spirit, one God, livest and reignest for ever.* Amen.